Meth & Speed =

Rich Mintzer

Enslow Publishers, Inc.

40 Industrial Road PO Box 38
Box 398 Aldershot
Berkeley Heights, NJ 07922 Hants GU12 6BP
USA UK

http://www.enslow.com

Library of Congress Cataloging-in-Publication Data

Mintzer, Richard.
   Meth & speed=Busted! / Rich Mintzer.
      p. cm. — (Busted!)
   Includes bibliographical references and index.
   ISBN 0-7660-2551-9
   1. Methamphetamine abuse—Juvenile literature. 2. Methamphetamine—Juvenile
literature. I. Title: Meth and speed=Busted!. II. Title. III. Series.
   HV5822.A5M56 2005
   613.8'4—dc22   2004027547

Printed in the United States of America

10 9 8 7 6 5 4 3 2 1

To Our Readers: We have done our best to make sure all Internet Addresses in this book were active and appropriate when we went to press. However, the author and the publisher have no control over and assume no liability for the material available on those Internet sites or on other Web sites they may link to. Any comments or suggestions can be sent by e-mail to comments@enslow.com or to the address on the back cover.

Illustration Credits: Associated Press, p. 10, 12, 22, 36; BananaStock, pp. 62–63, 69; Digital Stock, pp. 41, 71; Drug Enforcement Administration, pp. 4–5, 7, 8, 14, 19, 55, 57, 85; Enslow Publishers, Inc., pp. 24, 26; Hemera Technologies, Inc. 1997–2000, p. 39; © 2005 JupiterImages, pp. 46–47; LifeArt, p. 21; Rubberball, pp. 16–17; stockbyte, pp. 32–33, 74–75.

Cover Illustration: Associated Press

CONTENTS

CHAPTER ONE

DRUG BUST!

It was April 2003. Agents from the Drug Enforcement Administration (DEA) and members of the Royal Canadian Mounted Police (RCMP) had been in close contact for eighteen months. Together they had investigated the illegal importing of a chemical called pseudoephedrine from Canada into the United States.[1] The chemical, being smuggled across the border, is used in making the drug methamphetamine. The goal of the DEA agents was to cut off the supply of the chemicals to the meth labs in the United States and find out who was behind the illegal operation. The investigation, called Operation Northern Star, included police departments in ten cities across the United States and Canada. FBI agents were also helping to plan what would be one of the biggest drug busts in United States and Canadian history.[2]

Agents investigating the drug-transporting operation had found large quantities of the chemical pseudoephedrine in trailer trucks crossing the border, hidden beneath what were called "cover loads," which included boxes of chewing gum or bottled water. This is how the drug was being smuggled into the United States. The trucks carrying the chemical across the border would unload the contents, and the drug would then be stashed in secret hiding places in several cars. This allowed for the drug dealers to get the chemicals to people in a wider range of places. The agents watched and waited from secret locations as the traffickers transported the drugs.

The logo for Operation Northern Star.

They wanted to see where the drug was being transported and who was receiving it.

Once a list was compiled of numerous people involved in the drug trafficking, the bust was scheduled. Police, FBI, and DEA agents arrived, some with guns drawn, at private homes, offices, and meth labs. Quickly the officers entered the premises of more than a dozen locations, zeroed in on their suspects, slapped handcuffs on them, read them their rights, and led them to patrol cars that were waiting out front. On that day, a

Operation Northern Star targeted these cities.

total of sixty-five arrests were made in Detroit, Chicago, New York, Los Angeles, Cincinnati, Gulfport (Mississippi), and Riverside (California) in the United States as well as Montreal, Vancouver, and Ottawa in Canada.[3]

Included in the arrests were six executives who worked in three Canadian chemical companies. They were charged with selling major amounts of pseudoephedrine to the United States for the making of illegal methamphetamine.[4]

Michael J. Garcia, assistant secretary for the

Bureau of Immigration and Customs Enforcement, told newspaper reporters, "Operation Northern Star represents a great example of cross-border cooperation. Thanks to the joint efforts of United States and Canadian authorities, methamphetamine lab operators have been denied a huge source of chemicals used to make meth. This case should have significant impact on the ability of meth traffickers to make and sell their deadly product."[5]

Operation Northern Star was an example of a major drug bust. Agents and officers from many agencies teamed up and worked together. For a year and a half, they kept track of the locations where the chemicals were being shipped, tracked down where the meth labs were located, and made the bust. It is estimated that the pseudoephedrine would yield about 9,000 pounds of methamphetamine worth between $36 and $144 million.[6]

Drug Bust in Nevada

Not all drug busts cover as many states or include as many law enforcement agencies as Operation Northern Star. In fact, most are much smaller and are carried out by local law enforcement

Police officers and investigators often test for methamphetamine at a crime scene using special instruments and chemicals.

based on tips from anonymous callers who smell the chemicals or have knowledge that someone is making or selling methamphetamine, also called meth.

In late January 2003, the officers who make up the Consolidated Narcotics Unit (CNU) in Washoe County, Nevada, received a tip about a methamphetamine lab in the town of Sparks, Nevada.[7] The CNU is made up of officers from the Washoe County Sheriff's Office, Reno and Sparks police departments, and DEA agents, all of whom had special training in the area of narcotics.

Using unmarked cars and wearing civilian clothing, the unit visited the area and began looking for information about the lab and the operators. After four days of watching the location carefully, they followed two men leaving the building where the meth lab was reportedly located. They followed the two men into a casino in Reno, Nevada, where they observed them distributing one pound of meth to several people.

In 2001, over 100 people were arrested for illegal trafficking of pseudoephedrine, a key ingredient of methamphetamine. Operation Mountain Express III included the DEA, U.S Customs Service, Internal Revenue Service and the Royal Canadian Mounted Police.[8]

The state of Tennessee has its own task force to bust illegal methamphetamine labs.

The CNU officers immediately arrested both men and charged them with possession and sale of methamphetamine.[9]

They then searched the vehicle the men had been riding in and found nine more pounds of crystal methamphetamine hidden inside. Now having evidence that illegal drug trafficking was taking place, they got a search warrant and searched the location from which the two men had left. There they discovered a meth lab and another man who was making the drug. He was also arrested.[10]

Once narcotics agents discover a meth lab, they have to work quickly since labs can be easily picked up and moved to another location. In addition, because the chemicals are often very dangerous, agents and police officers need to be carefully trained in how to dismantle a meth lab so that they do not injure themselves or leave toxic waste behind.

The goal of drug busts such as Operation Northern Star is to keep methamphetamine out of the hands of potential users. Many users are starting to try the drug in their teens which can be very dangerous. According to the U.S. Department of Health and Human Services' *Results From the 2002 National Survey on Drug Use*

What Does Methamphetamine Look Like?

- **Meth is a white odorless powder that easily dissolves in water.**
- **Crystal meth, or ice, is clear chunky crystals.**
- **Yaba is in the form of small, brightly colored tablets.**

Operation Northern Star was a huge bust. This is a portion of the pseudoephedrine tablets they uncovered.

and Health: National Findings, more than 12 million people age twelve and older (5.3 percent) reported that they had used methamphetamine at least once in their lifetime. Other surveys show that nearly 10 percent of high school students have used meth during their years in high school.[11]

One of the problems that law enforcement agencies find is that as soon as they stop one source of illegal drug trafficking, there are reports of another source. They stay on top of each situation because of the potential harm of a drug such as methamphetamine.

Street Names for Methamphetamine

Beanies	Methlies Quik
Black Beauty	Motorcycle Crack
Blue Devils	Nazimeth
Chicken Feed	OZs
CR	Pink Elephants
Crink	Po Coke
Cristina	Poor Man's Cocaine
Crypto	Redneck Cocaine
Crystal Meth	Rock
Desogtion	Schmiz
Fast	Scootie
Geep	Spackle
Geeter	Speckled Birds
Getgo	Spoosh
Glass	Tick Tick
Granulated Orange	Trash
Ice	Yellow Bam
Meth	Yellow Powder

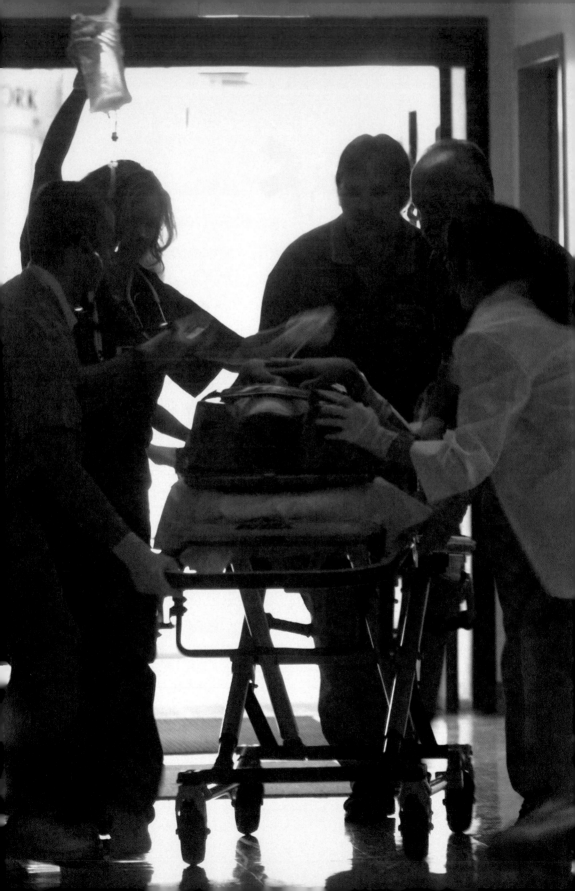

CHAPTER TWO

CRANK BUGS, METH MOUTH, & OTHER EFFECTS

Dr. Clifford Gervitz was working in the ER that evening. It was not a particularly busy night. He was near the end of his shift when Jeffery was brought in on a stretcher from the ambulance. Jeffery, a twenty-five-year-old graduate student, was taking methamphetamine to stay awake for exams. In the past, he had experienced some of the typical effects of the drug, including mood cycles and paranoia, but he kept taking it because without it he could not stay awake all night studying for his finals.[1]

This time, however, the drug had raised his blood pressure to twice its normal level.

He had collapsed and his friends had called an ambulance. The result was an aneurysm, which is the bursting of a blood vessel in the brain, resulting in internal bleeding. He was rushed into surgery. Life would never be the same again for Jeffery. It took doctors several hours, but they were able to stop the bleeding in Jeffery's brain and save his life.

Now, several years later, Dr. Gervitz, who is currently the medical director for the Addiction Recovery Institute (ARI) of New Rochelle in New York, still recalls the story as one of the saddest he had witnessed in his long medical career:

> Here you have a young healthy twenty-five-year-old young football player living in a nursing home and requiring round-the-clock care. He looks and moves like an eighty-five-year-old man. He can't even move half of his body; he's drooling from the mouth. Jeffery had his whole life ahead of him and now he has no cognitive functioning. Perhaps in fifty years he might

have had something like this happen anyway, but all he did was speed up the process.[2]

Methamphetamine is an illegal drug made in clandestine (secret) laboratories by the cooking of several chemicals together. Most of the chemicals can be purchased "over the counter," which means legally in stores. Once the chemicals are combined, they produce a white, odorless, bitter-tasting powder that can be taken in several ways, including smoking, snorting, or injecting into the

Methamphetamine can be made illegally with ingredients that are found in drug stores.

bloodstream. The drug can also be made into a chunky crystal-looking shape called crystal meth. On the street, crystal meth is often called ice because the clear quality makes it appear like a piece of ice. There are also colorful pills of methamphetamine known as yaba. Although the appearance differs, the results of taking any form of methamphetamine are similar.[3]

The makers of methamphetamine use either ephedrine or pseudoephedrine as one of the ingredients. When cooked, both drugs can leave poisonous gases in the atmosphere, making methamphetamine not only dangerous for users but also for the environment.[4]

Once someone starts using methamphetamine, the individual's brain does not want to stop the artificial "high" feeling that the drug creates, so it seeks more of the drug. This makes the drug very addictive, meaning when the person starts using meth, it becomes very hard to stop.[5]

What Is Methamphetamine and How Does It Affect the Body?

There are many effects methamphetamine can have on the body. Usually, it takes a very short time for someone to feel the initial effects of the drug, which can last from six to ten hours. The effects include a feeling of euphoria (or extreme happiness) and a sense of being very wide-awake and energetic. These are the reasons people take the drug, especially club-goers who want to stay up and dance all night. However, what the user does not realize is that the list of negative results of taking methamphetamine is much longer

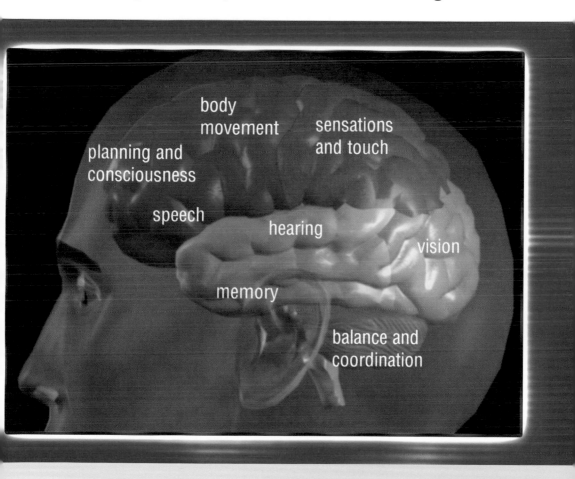

Drugs affect the way the brain behaves and the way it communicates with the rest of the body.

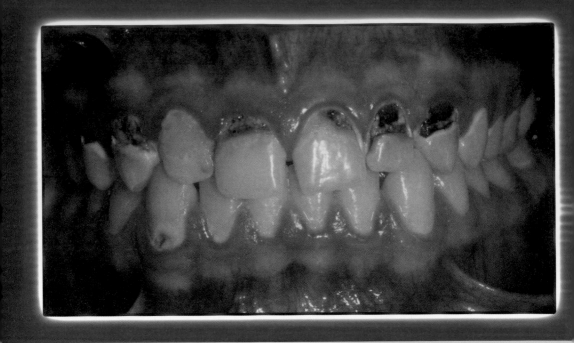

One of many side effects of methamphetamine use is the rotting of teeth. "Meth mouth" results from the user's body not being able to produce enough saliva.

and includes many serious consequences. Meth causes extreme nervousness, rapid heartbeat, dizziness, restlessness, insomnia (inability to sleep), severe depression, a rise in heart rate or blood pressure, and possibly even a stroke. Convulsions and an extreme rise in body temperature can also be a result. Body temperature for meth users has been reported as high as 108° F, which can kill a person. Long-term effects of methamphetamine use include insomnia, mental problems, rapid or irregular heart rate, or stroke. Overdoses can cause death.[6]

CRANK BUGS, METH MOUTH, & OTHER EFFECTS

The effects caused by injecting speed into the body can be more severe because the drug enters the bloodstream much faster. Along with the effects mentioned above, injecting speed makes the possibility of an overdose more likely. Sharing a syringe, or needle, can also cause the user to develop hepatitis B or C or HIV/AIDS.[7]

Once in the bloodstream, meth stimulates the release of adrenaline, which causes the blood pressure to increase and the heart rate to rise. Blood vessels constrict, or narrow, and the wind-pipes expand. Glucose, which is blood sugar, is then released into the bloodstream. These physical changes cause users to feel greater energy and alertness.

Methamphetamine releases high levels of dopamine, a chemical in the brain, which affects a person's mood and his or her body movements. It also damages neuron terminals, which carry information within the brain. Since the entire body is affected by the brain, when the drug gets there, it can cause many things to happen in other parts of the body. For example, a meth user may experience convulsions or have a hard time controlling a certain part of his or her body.[8]

The other major issue that comes from

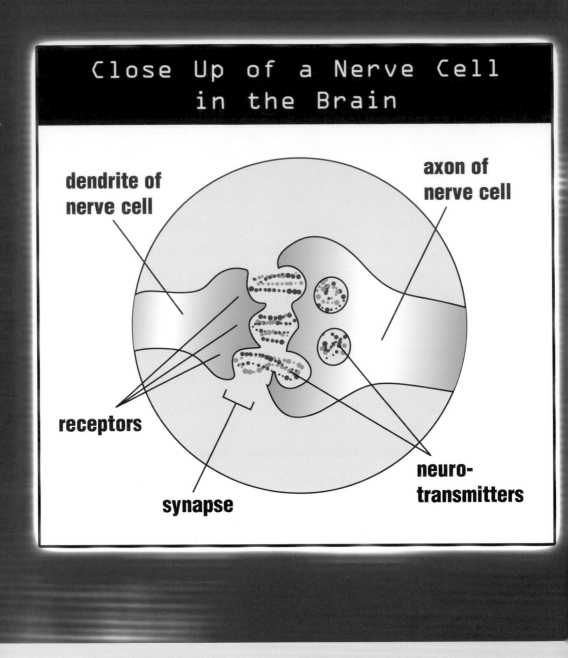

Close Up of a Nerve Cell in the Brain

dendrite of nerve cell

axon of nerve cell

receptors

synapse

neuro-transmitters

The brain has many nerve cells, or neurons. The parts of a neuron, the axon and dendrite, "talk" to each other using neurotransmitters. When a neuron wants to talk to another neuron, it releases neurotransmitters from its axon. The neurotransmitters cross the synapse and attaches to the dendrite of another neuron. When a person takes methamphetamine, or another drug, this process is interrupted and can cause the person to act in a different manner.

methamphetamine entering the brain is that it affects the individual's reward or pleasure area of the brain and throws everything off balance. In the brain there are areas that take in pleasure and other areas that handle the other important functions of our body. Methamphetamine takes attention away from the other needs of a person, such as the need to sleep and eat, and artificially focuses everything on the pleasure area. The body begins to crave the artificial pleasures sought by the drug instead of satisfying normal needs of life. In a scientific study, laboratory animals pressed levers so they could take methamphetamine.[9] Researchers saw that even with food available, the animals ignored all other activities, including eating, just because their brains became focused only on pleasure. As a result, they nearly starved to death before the tests were halted. Humans react in a similar manner, seeking more of the drug and staying awake for three or four days straight.

Someone craving meth, not unlike the animals tested, will completely ignore other parts of his or her life, including taking care of children. Once the effects of the drug wear off, humans crash. This means their body needs to catch up on normal

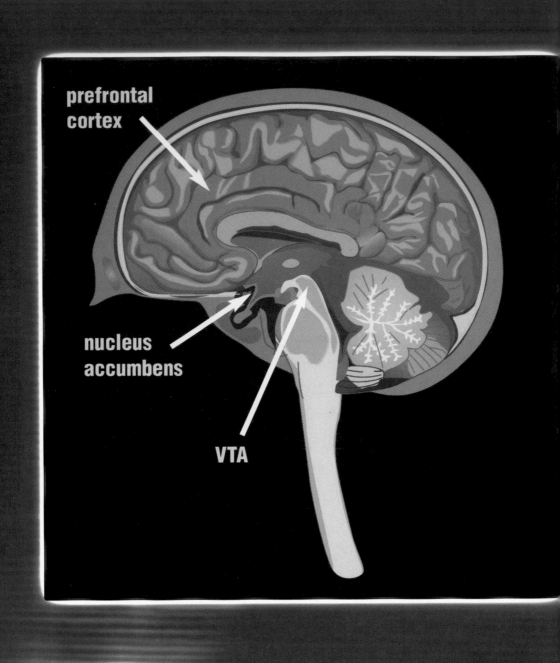

prefrontal
cortex

nucleus
accumbens

VTA

One part of the brain that is effected by drugs is the reward pathway. The reward pathway effects how a person feels. Several parts of the brain—the ventral tegmental area (VTA), the nucleus accumbens, and the prefrontal cortex—are activated by a rewarding stimulus such as food or water. The information travels from the VTA to the nucleus accumbens and up to the prefrontal cortex.

functioning, such as sleeping, which someone may do for many hours after coming off a meth binge.

Psychological Effects

People who use large amounts of methamphetamine for a long period of time may develop serious mental disorders. In many cases they will experience hallucinations, which is when a person sees images in his or her mind that he or she believes are real. In other instances, users will become paranoid. They may be suspicious and believe that other people are out to get them or harm them in some manner. Long-term emotional and behavioral symptoms also include severe depression and violent outbursts. Users can act in an unpredictable manner, especially when the body craves more of the drug.

As users develop a greater tolerance for the drug, they often try to intensify the experience by taking a higher dose or changing their means of taking the drug. Oral users, for example, may move to injection to get a faster high. After several hours, sometimes as many as eight, the drug begins to wear off and the crash begins to occur. Pleasure can turn into pain. As meth leaves the body, the user begins to feel anxious, irritable, and out of control.

Psychologically, the user does not want to come down from the high, an experience that becomes more painful and more difficult as the dosage increases. This is when some meth users may go on a binge. During a binge, the individual might take as much as a gram of meth every two or three hours to maintain a high for several days. Also known as a run, the person will often go without sleep for most of this time. Methamphetamine is an appetite suppressant, and the person feels so energetic that he or she does not feel a need to eat.

Chronic users also develop sores on their bodies from scratching at "crank bugs," which is a term used to describe the delusion that bugs are crawling under the skin. Such psychotic symptoms can sometimes persist for months after use has ceased.[10]

Withdrawal

Withdrawal symptoms for a methamphetamine user coming off the drug can include severe depression, anxiety, irritability, and a craving for the drug that can last for weeks or even many months.

Diet Pills and Speed

Methamphetamlne was once a key ingredient in diet pills because it stops people from feeling hungry. Unfortunately, many people taking diet pills became addicted and ended up in need of rehab programs to break the addiction they developed to the drug.[11]

A former meth addict describes the hopelessness and despair, "Withdrawal is the worst feeling I've ever felt. You feel like nothing. You cannot move without aching everywhere, and this is after one full week of sleep."[12]

People going through withdrawal are unable to work, attend school, or fulfill other necessary obligations. They are typically unable to make well-thought-out decisions and may act in a rash manner, sometimes endangering themselves, and other times endangering those around them.[13]

Tweakers

A tweaker is a methamphetamine addict who probably has not slept in three to fifteen days and is irritable and paranoid. A tweaker may be dangerous and behave in a violent manner.

At first look, a tweaker may appear normal. At closer observation, one can see that the tweaker's

Detecting a Speed User

There are several ways to tell if someone is using methamphetamine. Here are some that are easily recognizable.

- Constant movement and activity, including fidgeting, tapping feet, tapping fingers, and/or repetitive actions
- Excessive, often fast, talking
- Panic attacks
- Paranoia
- Aggressive, angry, and/or violent outbursts
- Inconsistent sleep patterns, such as staying up for a couple of nights, then sleeping for an extended amount of time
- Sudden, excessive weight loss
- Burns on their hands
- Disoriented "crazed look"
- Rotting teeth, "meth mouth"
- Sores, pimples, or scabs on arms, legs, neck, or face[14]

eyes are moving much faster than normal, the voice has a slight quiver, and his or her movements are quick and jerky.

The addict craves meth but cannot find a dosage that will suffice. Sometimes the tweaker is using alcohol or another drug to fill in where the meth is no longer having the desired effect. Law enforcement officers and medical staffers have a difficult time trying to calm down someone who is tweaking.

Police report that often tweakers are involved in car accidents, domestic disputes, or other violent activities. They may be picked up by the police for muggings, assaults, and other crimes in an attempt to get money to support their habit.[15]

The reality is that methamphetamine is a very potent and dangerous mixture of chemicals that can harm almost every major organ in the body; create an addiction; disrupt or destroy a family; cause someone to start lying, stealing, and acting in a violent manner; and release poisons to the environment. The many people who have not and will not take methamphetamine cannot help but wonder how or why anyone would put such a chemical mixture into his or her body.

CHAPTER THREE

THE HISTORY OF METHAMPHETAMINE

The drug methamphetamine was first synthesized in Japan in January 1919. It was actually a more compressed, stronger version of amphetamine that had first been created by German chemist L. Edeleano in 1887.[1]

The basis for the drugs amphetamine and methamphetamine is ephedrine, an organic substance from plants in the genus *Ephedra*. It has been used to treat asthma and colds in China for centuries.[2] In 1928, a U.S. pharmaceutical company started selling an amphetamine inhaler that could enlarge nasal and bronchial passages. Researchers also discovered that amphetamine acted as a stimulant, which means it provides people with added energy.[3] By the early 1930s, scientists began exploring various other uses for the drug. They discovered that it could be used as a means of raising blood pressure and helping people with a sleeping disorder called narcolepsy. The initial response to the medical and scientific findings was so positive that by 1928, amphetamines (made from ephedrine) were sold in drugstores under the name Benzedrine. These amphetamines could help hay fever and cold sufferers, as well as people with asthma. A condensed version of amphetamine, called methamphetamine, was found to be even stronger and was used in cold remedies marketed under the name Methedrine.[4]

The effects of methamphetamine, however, were greater than those of amphetamines. People began buying the drugs legally for reasons other than those that were intended by the manufacturer. For example, inhalers, which were supposed to help people breathe more easily, were broken open, and people would ingest the chemicals for an energizing effect.[5]

By the 1940s, World War II fighter pilots were using methamphetamine to help them stay awake on long missions. The drug was even nicknamed "The Awake Drug."[6]

In Japan, methamphetamine was also being used by soldiers during World War II. When the war ended, the remaining military supplies were turned over to the Japanese citizens. The first stimulant-addicted person was admitted to a hospital in Tokyo in September 1946. This was the beginning of a methamphetamine epidemic in Japan that lasted nearly twenty years.[7]

By the late 1950s, amphetamines were being prescribed by doctors for depression, obesity, and for other reasons. Methamphetamine tablets were being used for medical reasons, including breathing or respiratory problems, as well as for nonmedical reasons, such as staying awake for long periods of time or having extra stamina. By the early 1960s, methamphetamine abuse was on the rise in the United States, and it was also being abused by the American soldiers fighting

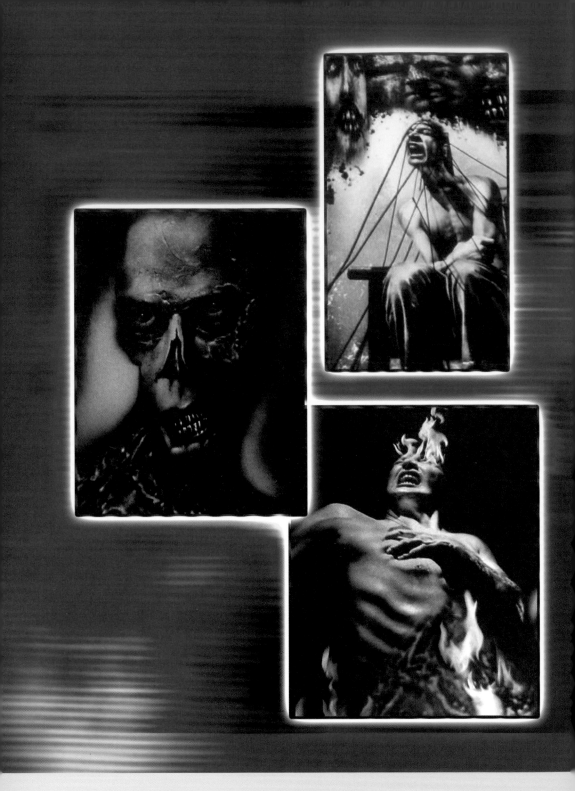

In an effort to portray the effects of methamphetamine use, these three images were used in a "Life or Meth" campaign.

in the Vietnam War, some of whom came home addicted to meth.[8]

One reason so many people were able to get drugs such as amphetamines and methamphetamine in the 1960s was that shipments of legitimately manufactured drugs were brought into the country for medical purposes. Gang members and drug dealers stole them from the trucks.[9]

In 1967, San Francisco was at the center of a new culture where many college students, some called hippies, were rebelling against the war taking place in Vietnam and other issues they opposed. There were very colorful designs on posters and clothing and innovative music. Unfortunately, this new culture began taking drugs in an attempt to escape the world around them. The most commonly used drugs were marijuana and LSD (lysergic acid diethylamide). Drug overdoses were reported on the news nearly every day, and many young people died or ended up in hospitals. Law enforcement agents, from the federal level to the local police departments, tried very hard to stop the possession and sale of these two drugs. In response, many of the users of these drugs moved over to methamphetamine.

It was still available in some cold medications and could be manufactured illegally by combining and cooking readily available chemicals in sinks and bathtubs. As the 1960s came to an end, the drug was very easy to get, and users were injecting the drug directly into the bloodstream for an immed-iate high.

The damaging effects of methamphetamine, also known as speed, were becoming widely known. Users were experiencing stomach cramps, shaking, anxiety, insomnia, paranoia, hallucinations, and stroke, and in the case of prolonged use, a number of deaths were report-ed. The slogan coined by the U.S. Department of Health in the mid-1960s, "Speed Kills" was prominently displayed on television ads, posters, and billboards in an attempt to spread the word about the dangers of speed. This media campaign, however, did not stop the increase in meth use.[10]

Finally, after the production and use of methamphetamine reached an all-time high at the end of the 1960s, the government passed the Comprehensive Drug Abuse Prevention and Control Act in 1970.

The new laws replaced and updated all previous laws concerning the use of illegal narcotics and

Law Enforcement

In 1970, methamphetamine was designated a Schedule II drug under the Controlled Substance Act, making possession and sale illegal except in specific medical situations. A Schedule II controlled substance has high potential for abuse but is currently accepted only for medical use in treatment in the United States. It may also lead to severe psychological or physical dependence.[11]

The Comprehensive Methamphetamine Control Act added new chemicals to the list of those restrictions in the production of methamphetamine in 1996. Penalties for manufacturing, selling, and trafficking were increased. Law enforcement could now seize such chemicals being used to make the drug.[12]

other dangerous drugs. They focused on law enforcement and imposed stricter penalties for anyone taking or selling illegal drugs. In addition, five classifications (called schedules) were set up, Schedule I being the most dangerous and Schedule V being the least dangerous drugs. The schedule of the drug was determined based on how dangerous it was, the potential for addiction, and whether it possessed any legitimate medical uses. The same classifications are used today.[13]

The new laws put an end to the growing epidemic of the drug by making medications that included amphetamine or methamphetamine either illegal or legal only through prescriptions. The law also made the chemicals used to make meth harder to obtain. The medical laboratories that still manufactured methamphetamine for medical reasons were now carefully monitored under strict government supervision. As a result, there was a significant drop in reported usage in the 1970s.[14]

Unfortunately, the new laws did not stop production and usage entirely. Illegal meth labs continued to originate primarily on the West Coast where the chemicals were more easily brought into the country illegally from Mexico and motorcycle gangs are more prevalent. Several motorcycle gangs became known as the leading distributors of the drug.

By the 1990s, however, meth was once again being made in numerous illegal West Coast labs. For many users it was a less expensive alternative to cocaine, which was a high-priced drug. Longer hours at work, greater pressures on teens and

Cocaine, along with methamphetamine, is an illegal and highly addictive drug.

young adults, plus peer pressure were also attributed to the return of the drug.[15]

In 1996, President Bill Clinton signed the Comprehensive Methamphetamine Control Act in response to what the DEA considered to be the fastest growing drug problem in the nation. The act is designed to help the DEA track down and investigate not only suspected drug users and dealers but also anyone suspected of buying the equipment and chemicals for the purpose of making methamphetamine. Many chemicals that can be purchased in stores would now be monitored so that a customer could not buy large amounts for the making of such illegal drugs. In addition, if someone was caught supplying laboratory equipment for illegal use, he or she could be fined heavily. It also increased penalties for trafficking in the chemicals and for possessing equipment to make the drug.[16]

Thanks to the new law, narcotics agents now had an easier time seizing the chemicals used to make meth. Statistics from 2001 show that authorities found and seized the drug in over fifteen hundred meth labs in California in that year alone. The problem, however, was that as fast as the authorities could find and destroy meth

The Methamphetamine Anti-Proliferation Act

In 2000, the Methamphetamine Anti-Proliferation Act was passed. This act helps train federal and state law enforcement officers on how to conduct methamphetamine investigations and the handling of the chemicals used in meth labs. It also expanded the efforts to stop the abuse of this dangerous drug by more carefully checking the contents and sizes of packages.[17]

labs, new ones popped up. Lab operators were finding new locations in which to make the drug, such as hotel rooms, rented spaces, toolsheds, the back of trucks, and even children's playrooms. The labs were easily portable and could be dismantled and moved very quickly. In addition, methamphetamine lab operators were now heavily armed, and the labs themselves were sometimes booby-trapped with explosives.[18]

What has made the return of methamphetamine even more difficult to curtail in recent years is that it is no longer primarily distributed by motorcycle gangs. The drug trafficking has now landed in the hands of organized crime, who have

How Does an Addict Use Meth?

- Injecting
- Snorting
- Smoking
- Oral ingestion

Source: Drug Enforcement Administration

a much larger network and can distribute methamphetamine to all parts of the country and many parts of the world. Members of crime families get methamphetamine through connections in Mexico where there is easy access to large amounts of ephedrine, the most important ingredient in the drug. In the United States, because of the use of ephedrine for manufacturing methamphetamine, the drug itself is illegal. There is an ongoing campaign continuing today to ban the inclusion of ephedrine in other medications because of the potential dangers seen in products mostly designed for weight loss.[19] Sometimes methamphetamine is made in Mexico and smuggled into the United States, while in other cases the chemical ephedrine is illegally brought into the United States, and the drug is then made in the labs. According to the DEA, in 2001 there were 12,715 methamphetamine laboratory incidents, ranging from fires to explosions to serious injuries to lab operators, reported in forty-six states.[20]

Today, methamphetamine trafficking and abuse in the United States have become a serious problem that is having a devastating impact on many communities across the nation. Families have been torn apart by meth addiction and even the environment has become at risk since the chemicals are very dangerous and often toxic.[21]

CHAPTER FOUR

METH: THE LAWS AND THE USERS

The drug bust occurred on a Saturday night in a club that had been watched by the police for several weeks. The local police had several reports of drug use. The people living in the area were concerned that the prevalence of meth in the clubs was changing their quiet southern California neighborhood.[1]

Sarah and Jill were arrested that night at the club. Sarah, twenty-one years old at the time, was charged with possession and sale of methamphetamine.[2] Jill was charged with being under the influence of methamphetamine.[3] The police officer who arrested Sarah found that she had a large amount of the drug on her. As they were handcuffed and led out of the club, officers immediately tested the drug by using a test tube and a solution that immediately identified that the drug was methamphetamine. Law enforcement agents in this area of California were prepared with several kits to test drugs during such a raid.

Both girls spent the night in jail.

Jill met with a substance abuse assessment officer, whose job was to determine if she was eligible for a substance abuse program. In the state of California, first-time offenders—individuals who were not considered serious drug users—can be eligible for what is called the PC 1000 program if the charge is either "possession of narcotics" or "being under the influence" of the drug. Jill qualified for the PC 1000 program. She would be ordered by the courts to a three-month drug education and rehabilitation program. Under the PC 1000 program, her charges would not be recorded in the police records at that time. If she completed the three-month program and then stayed out of trouble for the next eighteen months (which is what is called staying "clean"), the charges would be completely dropped, and it would be as if she had never been arrested.[4]

Sarah, however, was not eligible for the PC 1000 program or any other special program because she was also charged with sale of methamphetamine. According to California law, she was facing anywhere from sixteen months to four years in a state prison. Sarah's attorney told the court that Sarah was never actually seen distributing the drug, even though she had a substantial amount on her when she was arrested. He also told the judge that she held down a steady job and was a first-time offender. The court reduced her charge to possession only. This allowed her to be eligible for a rehabilitation program instead of facing time in prison.[5]

Sarah was sentenced under California Proposition 36 to nine months in an outpatient program and was assigned a probation officer to oversee her case. She would need to complete the program and stay clean for eighteen months. Her arrest was recorded, and the judge would determine after eighteen months, in conjunction with her probation officer and drug counselors, whether or not she would need to go for more treatment.

Eighteen months after completing the program, Jill remained clean and the charges were dropped. Sarah, however, returned to using methamphetamine. Her probation officer saw her and recognized the symptoms of meth use. Returning to court, she was ordered to a residential

The Substance Abuse and Crime Prevention Act, also known as Proposition 36, was passed by 61 percent of California voters on November 7, 2000. This law allows first- and second-time, nonviolent, drug possession offenders the opportunity to receive substance abuse treatment instead of going to jail. A total of $120 million annually for five and a half years is spent to pay for treatments services, which is less than sending the individual to prison.[6]

Recent studies have shown this program to be successful.

treatment center where she stayed for three months. Since leaving the residential treatment center, she has not violated her probation. She has been steadily assessed by her probation officer and drug counselors and has received random drug testing. While in the residential treatment facility, she learned new social skills so that when she left the treatment facility, she would not return to spending time with the people who influenced her to do methamphetamine.[7]

The state of California, because of the extremely high number of methamphetamine users, has enacted laws such as Proposition 36 and programs like PC 1000 in hopes of rehabilitating drug users rather than sending them to jail. Other states are not necessarily as lenient in their laws or may simply not be able to afford to start such programs and train people to run them. Methamphetamine use may mean jail time.

Marc Stevenson, program manager of PC 1000 East, at the McAlister Institute in El Cajon, California, also notes that California prisons are trying to help drug abusers. He states, "They have some prisons out here that have rehab centers and substance abuse programs within the prison facilities. Certain services are offered upon

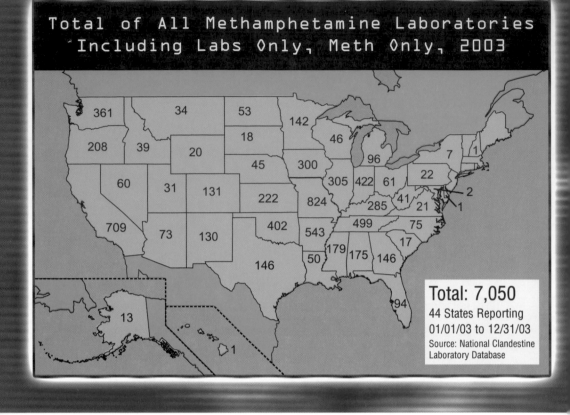

Total of All Methamphetamine Laboratories Including Labs Only, Meth Only, 2003

Total: 7,050
44 States Reporting
01/01/03 to 12/31/03
Source: National Clandestine Laboratory Database

release to help the individual develop a support network, find sober living housing, and so on. An effort is being made to help prevent people from going back to using meth."[8]

Keeping Law Enforcement Agencies Busy

In recent years, the making, selling, and usage of methamphetamine has kept federal and state agencies very busy. The nationwide Federal Drug Seizure System (FDSS) reportedly seizes over 2,000 kilograms of methamphetamine each year.

In 2000, the number topped 3,000 kilograms. According to the El Paso Intelligence Center's National Clandestine Laboratory Seizure System, 8,290 methamphetamine labs were seized in 2001. Another 303 "superlabs" were identified and destroyed throughout the United States, each with the capacity to produce ten or more pounds of methamphetamine in one production cycle.[9]

Many cities have put together special drug task forces and narcotics bureaus to help combat drug use. In cities and towns where methamphetamine use is high, special meth task forces are operating. Such a task force is usually comprised of members of the community and law enforcement officials. "They follow up on reports often given by people on the streets looking to get the meth," explains Marc Stevenson. "Cops also follow people who appear to be under the influence and are heading to labs to get more of the drug."[10]

Lab seizures are treated as toxic waste sites because of the poisonous chemicals used in the making of methamphetamine. Officers busting up such labs are specially trained in how to handle the potentially dangerous, explosive and toxic chemicals. In some cases, lab operators will set the lab on fire, allowing them time to escape and preventing the officers from getting to the meth.

In California, very sophisticated equipment is now being used by local police and drug task forces. Aircraft can detect signs of the chemicals coming out of a household or vacant building where a meth lab may be situated.

"Police also follow the cycle of the users," says Stevenson. "They will keep someone under surveillance while they are staying up on the drug, which can sometimes be a two- or three-day run. They wait until the person has to come down from the meth and then they make their move. At this point, the user crashes and can barely stay awake and function. It's easy for the police to move in at this time. In most cases the lab operators are also users, so they will also crash at some point."[11]

Special Training

The increase in meth labs has resulted in the Drug Enforcement Administration's need for a clandestine laboratory certification school. DEA agents and state and local police officers can train in the safest methods to raid and destroy a meth lab without causing injury to themselves or others.

In addition, they learn how to safely dispose of the chemicals found at these sites. Ways to determine that a lab is operating and how to investigate such illegal activities are also taught, along with how to recognize methamphetamine. While training, the agents and officers also take a rigorous eighty-four-hour physical fitness and defensive tactics course designed to prepare

Crystal Meth

them to prevail in all kinds of arrest scenarios. How to report the drugs and ways to handle meth users in a dignified and ethical manner are also part of the extensive training program. Over the past five years, eighteen hundred DEA special agents have graduated from the program.[12]

Along with national training such as the DEA program, many local law enforcement agencies have teamed up to create special meth task forces in what are called high-intensity drug-trafficking areas. The Fresno Methamphetamine Task Force, in Fresno, California, is an example of an effort by specially trained local and state law enforcement agents. Their goal is to stop meth sales and prevent chemical suppliers from getting the chemicals to the meth labs. Similar task forces are found in counties all throughout California and other states where methamphetamine is becoming a significant problem.[13]

One difficult scenario that many task force members face is how to deal with children at meth labs. Drug busts, particularly those of methamphetamine labs, can be terrifying scenes for children. Not only are there physical dangers from the chemicals in the lab, but also children may be taken away from their parents and placed in foster homes because their parents cannot take care of them while they are addicted to the drug.

In July 2001, officers raided a shed behind a house and arrested eight adults involved in making and selling methamphetamine. Three children were inside the house. Chemicals to make the drug were found hidden in their playroom, and the drug itself was found hidden inside of children's clothing.[14]

Drug raids bust methamphetamine makers and dealers. Bags like this are taken in as evidence.

Sometimes children are found near, or at, meth lab sites. Officers receive special training in how to bundle up the children and get them away from the crime scene safely. Typically, the children found at the meth labs in homes, backyards, or garages cannot even take toys with them when the police take them out of the house because the toys may have chemicals or drugs on them or inside of them.[15]

Who Uses Meth?

Police and law enforcement officials have tried to pinpoint where meth users are more likely to be found. Several national and many local agencies have gathered statistical research. Use of the drug crosses most ethnic, racial, and cultural lines. It is even used by a very wide age range, from kids as young as nine or ten to people in their forties and fifties.

According to the Substance Abuse and Mental Health Services Administration (SAMHSA) nearly 8 percent of high school seniors have tried methamphetamine at least once. The wide range of users discovered by SAMHSA surveys includes truck drivers who need to stay awake for long periods of time, factory and construction workers who need additional stamina, office workers doing overtime, people looking to lose weight, students studying all night for tests, and young adults going to late-night clubs and/or parties.[16]

While methamphetamine and cocaine both have serious effects, the people who take the two dangerous drugs are typically different. In fact, only 2 percent of users surveyed in several West Coast rehab clinics take both drugs.[17] Many meth users are former cocaine or crack users who have turned to meth as a substitute because the cost is lower. Among the most frequent users of the drug are truck drivers on long-haul deliveries who need to stay up for long periods of time.[18]

Where Is Methamphetamine a Major Problem?

According to the National Drug Intelligence Center (NDIC), methamphetamine is widely available throughout the Pacific, Southwest, and West Central regions and is becoming more commonly found in the Great Lakes and southeast parts of the country as well. In addition, law enforcement officials in Hawaii report that the use of the drug has reached dangerous numbers.

The Arrestee Drug Abuse Monitoring (ADAM) program listed thirty-six areas of the country with high percentages of adult arrestees testing positive for methamphetamine use. This includes arrests on other criminal charges where drug tests revealed methamphetamine in the bloodstream. In 2002, the percentages of adult male arrestees testing positive for methamphetamine in Honolulu, Hawaii, was 44.8 percent, followed by Sacramento, California (33.5 percent), San Diego, California (31.7 percent), and Phoenix, Arizona (31.2 percent). The highest percentages

Consequences of Methamphetamine and Amphetamine Use

- Addiction, psychotic behavior, brain damage.
- Chronic use can cause violent behavior, anxiety, confusion, insomnia, auditory hallucinations, mood disturbances, delusions, and paranoia.
- Damage to the brain caused by meth usage is similar to Alzheimer's disease, stroke, and epilepsy.

Source: Office of National Drug Control Policy and National Institute of Drug Abuse

of adult female arrestees testing positive for methamphetamine were located in Honolulu (50 percent), San Jose (42.8 percent), Phoenix (41.7 percent), Salt Lake City (37.7 percent), and San Diego (36.8 percent).[19]

According to the National Institute on Drug Abuse, meth use appears to be moving east. In 2002, nearly half of the 15,676 methamphetamine lab incidents, including fires and explosions were reported in nine middle-American states: Missouri, Iowa, Kansas, Oklahoma, Tennessee, Illinois, Arkansas, Kentucky, and Nebraska.[20]

Methamphetamine use poses a problem to law enforcement agencies, who are spending an increasing amount of time and money to try to stop the growing problem. They are working hard to find out who is using the drug and where the labs are in which it is being made. While there are fewer reports of meth use in eastern cities, some cities like New York and Boston have seen a slow increase in meth use among club-goers.

Therefore, people in all parts of the United States need to learn about both the physical dangers and the social problems caused by methamphetamine.

CHAPTER FIVE

REAL LIFE

Greg was from a poor family. They owned a farm and worked hard to keep it running. His dad was strict and did not allow him to do many typical things that kids enjoyed doing. He did not play baseball or learn to swim, and his family was too poor for him to have a bicycle. He worked hard at school, but when things did not go well or he did poorly on a test, his dad would get angry. In time, Greg started getting angry at himself. "I would become easily frustrated and sometimes wondered why bother trying at all," explains Greg. "I didn't have very high self-esteem."[1]

Then, when Greg was a teenager, two very traumatic experiences changed his life. First, he witnessed a young child getting killed in an accident. Then, his father became ill and died.

Feeling sad and depressed, Greg started drinking alcohol to try to feel better. "I liked the way alcohol made me feel, especially after working on the farm," says Greg.[2] After a while, it became clear that his family could no longer keep the farm running. They were out of money, and Greg and his mom lost the farm to pay off their debts.

Greg took jobs as a waiter, and when he was old enough, he took bartending jobs. He drank very often, but drinking was no longer making life feel better. Soon a friend introduced him to cocaine, and he liked that even better. Then he discovered meth, which was popular in the California town in which he grew up. "Meth was easy to get if you wanted it," recalls Greg. "All the kids in town knew someone who was selling the stuff. Then after doing meth a few times I wanted more. My body started wanting it, craving it."[3]

During the day, Greg was able to hold down his job as restaurant manager, and by night he would go to the popular dance clubs where drugs and alcohol were easy to find. Over the next several years, he found himself in trouble on several occasions. He was arrested seven times for possessing drugs, drunken driving, and once getting into a fight and putting his hand through a glass window. For that he needed forty stitches.

Greg recalls:

My family and the friends who weren't in the club crowd didn't know what to do to help me. My life was becoming a mess. Everything centered on getting the drug, until one night. I remember that night, I took a long look at myself in the mirror. It was four o'clock in the morning and I had another nosebleed . . . I got them all the time from the meth. Blood was dripping down my face onto my mustache and onto my T-shirt. My lower back hurt because there was blood passing though my kidneys. I looked at my face and my cheeks were sunken in. I looked like an old man and I thought I was going to die. I was sick, I was very tired, and I knew I had hit rock bottom.[4]

When Greg finally took that long look in the mirror, he realized most of the friends he had were not real friends but simply people who were doing meth with him or selling it to him. He realized that night that if he did not do something soon, he would not survive.[5]

"I started off in AA, Alcohol Anonymous, to help stop my drinking problem, and then I went for treatment to get myself off of meth," explains Greg. "It was very difficult to stop at first, but after a few months it got easier. I made sure I stayed away from anyone doing drugs. I wouldn't even date a woman who did drugs or drank."[6]

The longer Greg stayed away from people who influenced him in a negative way by doing drugs or drinking, the better he was able to build up confidence in himself. By going to a drug treatment center, he was able to talk with other people (also trying to stay off drugs), and they shared common experiences and the fears they had. "Knowing other people were going through exactly the same thing was very helpful," said Greg, about the treatment process, which included talking with counselors about how he felt not being on drugs.[7]

Greg's story has a happy ending. Today, fifteen

years since he last used meth, he is a counselor for a drug treatment house in California. He is able to use his own experiences to help others get over their addictions. However, the scar from punching a glass window and the list of arrests still remain as reminders of a very difficult time in his life.[8]

Barry, a good student, started hanging out with a bunch of kids that were doing meth during his senior year of high school. He got involved in meth, not just as a user but also as a seller, and eventually as a manufacturer in his own meth lab. "Instead of going on to college, I had a meth lab and for years I sold drugs to make money. I made a lot of money, but I knew I could get busted at any time."[9]

During his years selling methamphetamine, Barry got married and became the father of three children. "We remained isolated from other people, except those that I was selling to. I hardly had time for my kids and I regret that very much now," says Barry, whose social world revolved around meth and meth users. "Our whole world was centered around drugs and dealers. My wife got addicted to heroin during this time," adds Barry.[10]

With both parents heavily into drugs, Barry's oldest daughter, age ten, was now taking care of the younger daughter who was five. She made sure her younger sister was fed and clean. "At only ten years old, she felt responsible for her younger sister at all times and would have panic attacks if she didn't know exactly where she was at all times," says Barry.[11]

Meanwhile, Barry's oldest child, his son, wanted to follow in his father's footsteps. By the time he was thirteen, he was dealing drugs. He learned all about the illegal drug business from his dad, who did not want him to get involved but also was unable to stop him. Unlike Barry, who had eluded the police for eighteen years, his son got arrested and went to prison, where he would spend eight years.[12]

Finally seeing what the drugs were doing to the family, Barry's wife took their daughters to her mother's house and went to get help at a rehab center. Alone, without his daughters, his son in jail, and his wife in a rehab center, Barry finally realized what he had done to his family. He went to get help. At this point the police caught up with him. They did not catch him selling drugs, but they knew he had a lot of money

Drug dealers may think they are safe, but they eventually get caught.

and could not explain where it had come from. He was put under house arrest for a year and lost the money he had made illegally. He was only allowed out of his home to get treatment for his meth addiction.

For Barry, finding a job was not easy. "I had been smuggling drugs for eighteen years. I had no work history and no skills. I didn't know what to do for work or where to even look for a job. Who would want to hire me? Finally, I was able to start working in an adult detox center, helping adults get over their addiction, like I had done."[13]

Since then, Barry has gone on to manage a center that helps teens and adolescents get off drugs. His wife was able to get a job in the courts. They are still together after twenty-eight years, and the oldest children are now in their twenties and have jobs as well. Their youngest daughter, now seventeen, has reportedly stayed away from drugs.

Barry regrets terribly what his family had to go through because of his addiction and his years as a drug manufacturer and smuggler. "I really miss that I wasn't there for them when they grew up," says Barry, "I feel very guilty about that."[14]

Greg destroyed many years of his own life,

Sometimes it takes an arrest and jail time for an addict to realize he or she has a drug problem and needs to get help.

Secret, and Hazardous, Laboratories

Just like the drug has effects on the people who use them, the labs also have an effect on the environment. The production of one pound of methamphetamine releases poisonous gas into the atmosphere and creates five to seven pounds of toxic waste. Many laboratory operators dump the toxic waste down household drains or in fields and yards where children can accidentally discover the dangerous materials.[15]

while Barry took his family down with him. Fortunately, both stories had happy endings. However, there are many regrets and many lost years. Barry is thankful that he was able to find work, any kind of work. Even today his oldest daughter always wants to know if the younger daughter is OK, where she is going, and what she is doing. It is hard for her to break that habit after having to take care of her when they were kids and their parents were unable to be there for them.

Besides what meth can do to a person's social life and how it can destroy his or her family, it can put a person in trouble with the law. Greg was arrested seven times and Barry just once.

Many stories of meth users include not only how the drug was harmful physically, but also how it was damaging to families and personal relationships. Often, the friends of a meth user are other users, which makes it even more difficult to see how it is affecting the person's family and other people close to them.

Fortunately, people like Barry and Greg have joined the ranks of counselors helping people who are having problems breaking the methamphetamine addiction.

CHAPTER SIX

GETTING HELP

Between 1994 and 2000, the number of people admitted into special programs to help get over methamphetamine addiction doubled. Since 2000, the number has continued to rise. There are many counselors working hard in drug treatment facilities helping others to get over his or her addiction to this drug.

75

Such treatment is typically paid for either by the state, city, or county; by donations; or by the individuals seeking help (from their medical insurance), depending on the facility and who runs it.[1]

According to Greg, a former addict, who is now clean and helping others by working at a drug treatment center as a certified addiction specialist, "We don't give people other medications to get over their addiction to meth. We use what is called a social model treatment, which means the person starts by talking with people to help them understand that they have a problem. Then we try to get them to understand how they feel and what makes them feel the need to use the drug."[2]

Tammy Van Ness, director at McAlister Institute, in El Cajon, California, explains the process used at their drug treatment facility:

> A lot of the clients who come into treatment are here because somebody sent them, either their family or a judge. First the person will fill out paperwork to give the counselors some information on his or her background. Then the treatment counselors will determine the needs of the individual. They will determine how long they feel the person will need to be

in treatment, what program he or she will be in, and how often they will come for their treatment. Usually this is based on how long the person has been using the drug and how recently they last used it. If they've been using in the past thirty days we will usually ask them to come in three to five times a week.[3]

A treatment plan may include what is called a twelve-step program, where each step is another way of helping the person learn why he or she uses the drug and how he or she can find other ways to deal with his or her problems. A person must complete one step in the program before moving on to the next. "We encourage the person to get started in the twelve-step program and to get a sponsor, which is someone to help them work on the program," says Van Ness.[4]

Treatment also includes giving people education and having them get into a process group, which is where people talk about issues going on in their life. Many feelings come out during such discussions, and the people in the group may talk about the struggles they have staying off drugs. "In addition, everyone is assigned a counselor while they are in treatment and they can come in and do one-on-one discussions with the counselor," adds Van Ness.[5]

There is also random drug testing while people are in drug rehabilitation programs. This is to make sure they are staying off drugs. If people test positive, meaning they are still using drugs, the facility will take action. If it is a facility for people to meet after being off drugs, they will likely have to leave and return only when they are clean. If, however, it is a facility where people are still working on getting off drugs, the person may need a more immediate form of treatment. There are many types of treatment options available for every level from someone trying to break the addiction to people who have been off drugs for months and are trying hard to stay away from methamphetamine.

Among the activities that are also part of drug treatment are:

- Behavioral Intervention. This is a means of trying to change a person's way of thinking and his or her behavior so that he or she does not have to resort to taking the drug. The more someone learns how to deal effectively with situations that occur in life, the less dependent he or she will be on the drug.

- Family Counseling. In this case, other members of the family, who are very much affected by a person's meth addiction, can discuss how to deal with the problem in a way that is supportive and helpful.
- Network Therapy. This is where the individual receives therapy and develops a network of stable, nonsubstance-abusing support persons, such as family, partners, and close friends.[6]
- Emergency Room Treatment. This treatment focuses on overdoses by treating immediate symptoms of hyperthermia (elevated body temperature) and convulsions.

Greg also explains that people in treatment for methamphetamine use and other drugs need to learn to make new friends and try to fit in with a different crowd. "The peers of a drug addict are usually also either drug addicts, dealers, or involved with drugs in some manner. The less someone associates with such individuals, the more the person can break away from that lifestyle," says Greg.[7]

Getting Help

More often than not, methamphetamine users seek out help because someone has either strongly recommended that they do so or the courts have mandated it. Counselors such as Greg and Barry have seen parents bring teens or adolescents for help. They have also seen teens bring parents for help. "This is a drug that can affect people of many different ages. But no matter who comes in for help, the person has to really want to be helped for any kind of intervention to be possible," says Barry.[8]

Many people today, unsure where to find help for a family member or a friend, will turn to the Internet. Even users themselves have made efforts to get help through the Internet. According to the *Official Patient's Sourcebook on Methamphetamine Dependence*, many people today rely on the Internet for research, but as the National Institute of Health warns, some Web

If you know someone who may be addicted to methamphetamine, or any other drug or alcohol, urge that person to stop and get help. If that person is you, then do not take another chance with your life. Talk to an adult you trust, like a parent, teacher, or counselor, and get help.

sites provide valuable information while others are misleading. Patients often visit their doctors, carrying printed Web pages of home remedies. This has become so common that doctors often spend more time explaining that the information is incorrect than they do guiding patients through positive steps toward stopping their dependence on methamphetamine.[9]

Treatment centers for substance abuse (which includes methamphetamine use) are found in every state in the nation as well as in other countries. Some treatment centers provide residential care, but most can only afford to provide day treatment. Many different types of programs are included, most of which include group meetings and counseling. Some, however, include hypnosis or behavior therapy (working on changing how people behave).

Most treatment centers are run by experts in the field including doctors, social workers, nurses, psychologists, and other individuals trained in how to help people with drug problems and addiction.[10]

It is the hope of many individuals that more drug treatment centers will be opened so that fewer people will be sent to prison as a result of a minor crime committed because of their addiction. According to the National Institute on Chemical Dependency, it costs taxpayers $64,000 to house a nonviolent drug user in jail for a year, while it would cost only $26,000 to house a parent and two children in a treatment center for the same amount of time. In addition, they point out that nearly 79 percent of the drug users who go to prison return to using the drugs once they get out.[11]

Carefully Planned Treatment

To organize treatment strategies, it can be helpful to view the treatment process as consisting of

- A treatment initiation period, which is a time when the individual learns what the treatment program will consist of.
- An abstinence attainment period, where the person tries to reach a goal of abstinence, staying away from the drug.
- An abstinence maintenance phase, which is where the person stays off the drug for a period of time.
- A long-term abstinence support plan, meaning that other people are available

to help and support the individual who is staying off the drug.[12]

Bill Myers, a former meth addict, now a drug treatment outreach specialist in southern California, says that in some ways going for treatment is almost like being a baby. "Just like a baby learns to walk without holding on, people need to learn to do things all over again without the need for the drug to help them," says Myers.[13]

Preventing a Relapse

Sometimes people who have gone through treatment for taking methamphetamine have a relapse where they start taking the drug again. In some cases, they take it once and realize they need to get help quickly. In other situations, they hang out with friends who use the drug often and get addicted all over again. Drug counselors work hard to try to prevent relapses.

Relapse prevention teaches people:
- How to cope with the craving for the drug
- How to say no when offered meth
- How to cope with problems and try to solve them rather than turn to drugs
- How to apply some of what they learned in rehabilitation counseling to prevent a

major relapse so they do not become addicted all over again.[14]

Another reason some people slip into relapse is because once they are in recovery, addicts become amazed at how much spare time they have. After quitting drugs, they need activities to take the place of the time they spent looking to buy drugs, the time they were on the drug, and the time they spent coming down from the drug (crashing). It is important for people in recovery to find other things they like to do. If they list activities and try to find something of interest, perhaps something they did before becoming addicted, it is more likely they will avoid a relapse.[15]

A Story of Relapse

"When you go through rehab treatment, you are given a set of rules to use to stay clean. Many people in recovery have a habit of thinking they are different and can hang out with people who use drugs or get involved in a relationship with someone doing a drug like methamphetamine and not be affected by that relationship. It's very hard to do, even after going through recovery," says Van Ness.[16]

Van Ness describes her own relapse, after going through a treatment program.

From my own experience, because I hung out with people who were using meth and I was around these people all the time, after a while I began using meth all over again. But it was different, because I had experienced a taste of recovery and knew I could do better. I got very depressed when I went back on meth. I saw my child being exposed to my behavior.

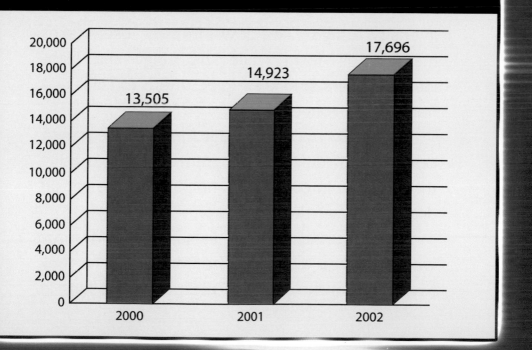

Emergency Department Drug Mentions—Methamphetamine

- 2000: 13,505
- 2001: 14,923
- 2002: 17,696

I knew it was unhealthy, so I thought about what my options were. What was I going to do? Give up my child? Kill myself? Go back to recovery? Having seen that recovery could work, I decided to go back and start the twelve-step program all over again. Finally, I did it, and returned to where I wanted to be. Now, I've been clean for fifteen years.[17]

Treating methamphetamine users means understanding the stages of use and the terminology used. Counselors have to know what is going on in the life of a meth addict so they can help them. Many counselors are former addicts, so they are familiar with the stages and terms.

Meth addiction starts with low-intensity usage, followed by bingeing, and then goes to high-intensity usage. The low-intensity user takes meth in pill form while the binge and high-intensity users smoke or inject meth to achieve a faster and stronger high.

There are many different kinds of treatment centers with different programs. The one thing they all have in common is helping people get off drugs and over their addiction.

Drug counselors such as Greg and Tammy work hard at treatment centers because they have been in the shoes of the people walking in

Terminology Counselors Learn

rush—This is the initial exuberant feeling the user gets when smoking or injecting the drug. The user's heartbeat races, and his or her blood pressure and pulse soar. A meth rush can last for five to thirty minutes.

high—This is the feeling after the rush where the user feels smarter and sometimes becomes argumentative. He or she is eager to talk and often interrupts people and even finishes their sentences for them. This may last from six to ten hours.

binge—This is where the user wants to continue the high and will do whatever is necessary to get more of the drug to continue to smoke or inject the drug whenever it feels as if it is wearing off. The rush, however, is shorter and not as strong as the first rush. In time, the user no longer feels the rush, but the user becomes hyperactive, both mentally and physically. A binge can go on for three days to nearly two weeks.

tweaking—This is a very dangerous time at the end of the binge where no matter what the user does, he or she is coming down from the high and feeling depressed and empty inside. Users try to stop the bad feelings but cannot, so some take other drugs or alcohol.

crash—To a binge abuser, the crash means an incredible amount of sleep. The body's epinephrine has been depleted, and the body uses the crash to replenish its supply. The crash can last one to three days.

normal—This is when the user returns to a state that is similar to where he or she was before taking the meth. As an addict binges more often, he or she experiences less of this state. Each time "normal" functioning returns, the addict is slightly more deteriorated than he or she was before the latest binge.[18]

to get help and know how tough a life it can be. Greg says that although he enjoys helping people, he is also thinking of other things he can do now that he has been off meth for sixteen years. He says he is happy to be one of the ones who made it through treatment successfully and stayed clean. "So many people don't," adds Greg, "especially the younger ones. It's too bad, because they don't realize how much time they are wasting."[19]

GLOSSARY

abstinence—The practice of abstaining from, or not doing, something.

controlled substance—Chemical substances that are controlled by the government, in regard to sale and usage, under the Controlled Substances Act.

convulsions—Involuntary muscle spasms or a series of spasms.

epidemic—An infection or health hazard that spreads rapidly and over a wide area.

hormone—A substance produced within the body tissues and transmitted through the bloodstream to send a message to another body tissue to affect physiological activity such as growth.

inhaler—A device that produces a vapor to help ease nasal congestion.

intensify—To make something stronger or more powerful.

outpatient program—A treatment program in which a person may come and go on a daily basis.

paranoia—A mental disorder where a person does not trust anyone and believes that other people are out to harm him or her.

potent—Having a strong or powerful effect.

psychotic—A person suffering from psychosis, which is a mental disorder where a person loses touch with reality and his or her normal functioning begins to deteriorate.

rehabilitation program—A program designed to rehabilitate someone or bring the individual back to good health.

relapse—To slip back into an old habit or way of acting, such as returning to doing drugs again after having stopped.

residential treatment center—A situation where patients are living at the center and receiving treatment.

speed—Slang term for methamphetamine and similar drugs.

toxic waste—Poisonous waste materials, typically involving chemicals, that can be hazardous to people or animals.

traffickers—Individuals conducting illegal or improper commercial activity, such as buying, selling, or trading drugs.

CHAPTER NOTES

Chapter 1. Drug Bust!

1. Ronald J. Hansen, "Fed Bust Meth Ring At Border," *Detroit News*, April 16, 2003, <http://www.detnews.com/2003/metro/0304/17/c01-138726.htm> (April 22, 2004).
2. Ibid.
3. Ibid.
4. Ibid.
5. Ibid.
6. Ibid.
7. Drug Enforcement Agency, Press Release, January 29, 2003, <http://www.dea.gov> (April 27, 2004).
8. "More Than 100 Arrested in Nationwide Methamphetamine Investigation," Transcript of News Release, DEA, January 10, 2002, <http://www.usdoj.gov/dea/major/me3.html> (May 16, 2005).
9. Drug Enforcement Agency, January 29, 2003.
10. Ibid.
11. Ibid.

Chapter 2. Crank Bugs, Meth Mouth, & Other Effects

1. Personal interview with Dr. Clifford Gervitz, medical director for the Addiction Recovery

Institute (ARI), New Rochelle, New York, April 7, 2004.

2. Ibid.

3. "Methamphetamine & Amphetamines," n.d., <http://www.gov/convern/meth_factsheet.html> (November 27, 2004).

4. Ibid.

5. Ibid.

6. Jennifer Lloyd, "November 2003," Drug Policy Information Clearinghouse Fact Sheet, Executive Office of the President, Office of National Drug Control Policy, November 2003, <http://www.whitehousedrugpolicy.gov/publications/factsht/methamph> (December 6, 2004).

7. Ibid.

8. Koch Crime Institute, "Methamphetamine Frequently Asked Questions," n.d., <http://www.kci.org/meth_info/faq_meth.htm> (May 14, 2004).

9. Koch Crime Institute, "What Is Crystal Methamphetamine?," n.d., <http://www.kci.org/meth_info/sites/meth_psycho.htm> (November 24, 2004).

10. Katherine Ketcham and Nicholas A. Pace, M.D., *Teens Under The Influence: The Truth About Kids, Alcohol and Other Drugs—How to Recognize the Problem and What to Do About It* (New York: Ballantine Books, 2003), pp. 144–145.

11. "More About Diet Pills," *Diet Pills*, n.d., <http://www.ecureme.com/emyhealth/data/Diet_Pills.asp> (June 8, 2005).

12. Ketcham and Pace, pp. 148–149.

13. Ibid.

14. Ketcham and Pace.

15. Addiction-Help Drug Prevention and Rehabilitation Center, "Methamphetamine Addiction & Side Effects," <http://www.drug-rehab-addiction-treatment.com/methamphetamine.html> (December 9, 2004).

Chapter 3. The History of Methamphetamine

1. Katherine Ketcham and Nicholas A. Pace, M.D., *Teens Under The Influence: The Truth About Kids, Alcohol and Other Drugs—How to Recognize the Problem and What to Do About It* (New York: Ballantine Books, 2003), p. 135.

2. June Weintraub, "Adverse Effects of Botanical and Non-Botanical Ephedrine Products," Harvard School of Public Health Drugs & Devices Information Line, 1997, <http://www.hsph.harvard.edu/Organizations/DDIL/ephedrine.html> (December 1, 2004).

3. Wikipedia, The Free Encyclopedia, "Benzedrine," December 6, 2004, <en.wikipedia.org/wiki/Benzedrine> (December 7, 2004).

4. National Institute of Drug Abuse, "History of Methamphetamine," January 1998, <http://

www.methamphetamineaddiction.com/
methamphetamine_hist.html#early> (May 14,
2004).

5. Ibid.

6. Ketcham and Pace, p. 137.

7. M. Tamura, "Japan: Stimulant Epidemics Past
and Present," reprint in United Nations Office
on Drugs & Crime, Bulletin on Narcotics,
1989,   <http://www.unodc.org/unodc/en/
bulletin/bulletin_1989-01-01_1_page007.
html#bf02> (December 7, 2004).

8. National Institute of Drug Abuse, "History of
Methamphetamine," January 1998, <http://
www.methamphetamineaddiction.com/
methamphetamine_hist.html#early> (May 14,
2004).

9. Elizabeth   Connell   Henderson,   M.D.,
Understanding   Addiction   (Jackson,   Miss.:
University of Mississippi Press, 2000), p. 58.

10. CBC News Indepth, "Crystal Meth FAQs,"
August 26, 2004, <http://www.cbc.ca/news/
background/drugs/crystalmeth.html>
(December 6, 2004).

11. " Methamphetamine," ONDCP Drug Policy
Information Clearinghouse Fact Sheet, November
2003,   <http://www.whitehousedrugpolicy.
gov/publications/factsht/methamph/> (May 16,
2005).

12. Ibid.

13. U.S. Drug Enforcement Administration, 1996,

<http://www.usdoj.gov/dea/agency/csa.htm>
(May 17, 2005).

14. National Institute of Drug Abuse, "History of Methamphetamine," January 1998, <http://www.methamphetamineaddiction.com/methamphetamine_hist.html#early> (May 14, 2004).

15. Ibid.

16. U.S. Drug Enforcement Administration, "The History of the DEA from 1973 to1998," n.d., <http://www.usdoj.gov/dea/pubs/history/> (May 16, 2004).

17. "Methamphetamine Anti-Proliferation Act of 2000 (MAPA)," Office of Diversion Control, n.d., <http://www.deadiversion.usdoj.gov/chem_prog/faqs/mapa_faq.htm> (May 16, 2005).

18. Jennifer Lloyd, "November 2003," Drug Policy Information Clearinghouse Fact Sheet, Executive Office of the President, Office of National Control Policy, November 2003, <http://www.whitehousedrugpolicy.gov/publications/factsht/methamph> (May 18, 2004).

19. June Weintraub, "Adverse Effects of Botanical and Non-Botanical Ephedrine Products," Harvard School of Public Health, 1997, <http://www.hsph.harvard.edu/Organizations/DDIL/ephedrine.html> (May 17, 2005).

20. Jennifer Lloyd, "November 2003," Drug Policy Information Clearinghouse Fact Sheet, Executive Office of the President, Office of

National Control Policy, November 2003, <http://www.whitehousedrugpolicy.gov/publications/factsht/methamph> (May 18, 2004).

21. Ibid.

Chapter 4. Meth: The Laws and the Users

1. Personal interview with Marc Stevenson, program manager of PC 1000 East, East County Regional Recovery Center, El Cajon, California, May 28, 2004.
2. Ibid.
3. Ibid.
4. Ibid.
5. Ibid.
6. Josh Richman, "Drug Treatment Law Gets High Marks, First Study of Prop. 36," *Oakland Tribune*, Thursday, July 17, 2003, <http://www.drugreform.org/news.tpl?action=2&newsid=105846967522061> (May 17, 2005).
7. Personal interview with Marc Stevenson, program manager of PC 1000 East, East County Regional Recovery Center, El Cajon, California, May 28, 2004.
8. Ibid.
9. Jennifer Lloyd, "November 2003," Drug Policy Information Clearinghouse Fact Sheet, Executive Office of the President, Office of National Control Policy, November 2003,

<http://www.whitehousedrugpolicy.gov/ publications/factsht/methamph> (May 29, 2004).

10. Personal interview with Marc Stevenson, program manager of PC 1000 East, East County Regional Recovery Center, El Cajon, California, May 28, 2004.

11. Ibid.

12. U.S. Drug Enforcement Administration, "Clandestine Laboratory Training," n.d. <http://www.usdoj.gov/dea/programs/ training/part17.html> (May 22, 2004).

13. "Central Valley HIDTA," White House Drug Policy, High Intensity Drug Trafficking Areas, n.d., <http://www.whitehousedrugpolicy.gov/ hidta/centvalley-content.html> (May 24, 2004).

14. Ibid.

15. Bethany Clough, "Youth Among Meth's Victims: Drug Busts Result in Fright and Loss of Home for Children of Meth Users, Makers," *Sacramento Bee*, September 2, 2002.

16. Substance Abuse and Mental Health Services Administration, n.d., <http://www.samhsa.gov> (June 2, 2004).

17. Personal interview with Tammy Van Ness, program manager, East County Regional Recovery Center, El Cajon, California, June 1, 2004.

18. Elizabeth Connell Henderson, M.D., *Understanding Addiction*, (Jackson: University of Mississippi Press, 2000), pp. 58–59.

19. Jennifer Lloyd, "November 2003," Drug Policy Information Clearinghouse Fact Sheet, Executive Office of the President, Office of National Control Policy, November 2003, <http://www.whitehousedrugpolicy.gov/publications/factsht/methamph> (June 4, 2004).
20. National Institute on Drug Abuse, "Info Facts," September 18, 2004, <http://www.nida.nih.gov/Infofax/methamphetamine.html> (May 17, 2005).

Chapter 5. Real Life

1. Personal interview with Greg X., California, June 8, 2004.
2. Ibid.
3. Ibid.
4. Ibid.
5. Ibid.
6. Ibid.
7. Ibid.
8. Ibid.
9. Personal interview with Barry X., California, June 11, 2004.
10. Ibid.
11. Ibid.
12. Ibid.
13. Ibid.
14. Ibid.
15. Jennifer Lloyd, "November 2003," Drug Policy Information Clearinghouse Fact Sheet,

Executive Office of the President, Office of National Control Policy, November 2003, <http://www.whitehousedrugpolicy.gov/publications/factsht/methamph> (June 12, 2004).

Chapter 6. Getting Help

1. Jennifer Lloyd, "November 2003," Drug Policy Information Clearinghouse Fact Sheet, Executive Office of the President, Office of National Control Policy, November 2003, <http://www.whitehousedrugpolicy.gov/publications/factsht/methamph> (June 14, 2004).
2. Personal interview with Greg X., California, June 8, 2004.
3. Personal interview with Tammy Van Ness, program manager, East County Regional Recovery Center, El Cajon, California, June 4, 2004.
4. Ibid.
5. Ibid.
6. Ibid.
7. Personal interview with Greg X., California, June 8, 2004.
8. Personal interview with Barry X., California, June 11, 2004.
9. James N. Parker, M.D., and Philip M. Parker, Ph.D., *The Official Patient's Sourcebook on Methamphetamine Dependence: A Revised and Updated Directory for the Internet Age* (San Diego, Calif.: Icon Health Publications, 2002).

10. Personal interview with Greg X., California, November 23, 2004.

11. "Spend Funds on Family Residential Treatment Centers," n.d., <http://www.ni-or.com/treatment.html> (November 29, 2004).

12. Crystal Recovery, "Mission Statement," n.d., <http://www.crystalrecovery.com> (June 7, 2004).

13. Personal interview with Bill Myers, East County Regional Recovery Center, El Cajon, California, May 28, 2004.

14. "Relapse Prevention," National Guidelines Clearinghouse, an initiative of the U.S. Department of Health and Human Services, December 18, 2001, <http://www.guideline.gov/summary/summary.aspx?doc_id=2540> (June 7, 2004).

15. Cindy Mogil, *Swallowing a Bitter Pill* (Far Hills, N. J.: New Horizon Press, 2001), pp. 95–96.

16. Personal interview with Tammy Van Ness, El Cajon, California, June 1, 2004.

17. Ibid.; Personal interview with Greg X., California, November 23, 2004.

18. Jennifer Lloyd, "November 2003," Drug Policy Information Clearinghouse Fact Sheet, Executive Office of the President, Office of National Control Policy, November 2003, <http://www.whitehousedrugpolicy.gov/publications/factsht/methamph> (June 12, 2004).

19. Personal interview with Greg X., California, November 23, 2004.

FURTHER READING

Aretha, David. *Methamphetamines and Amphetamines*. Berkeley Heights, N. J.: MyReportLinks.com Books, 2005.

Fitzhugh, Karla. *Crystal Meth and Other Amphetamines*. Chicago, Ill.: Heinemann, 2005.

Littell, Mary Ann. *Speed and Methamphetamine Drug Dangers*. Berkeley Heights, N. J.: Enslow Publishers, Inc., 2000.

Schleifer, Jay. *Methamphetamine: Speed Kills (Drug Abuse Prevention Library)*. New York: Rosen Publishing Group, 1998.

Youngs, Bettie B., Jennifer Leigh Youngs, and Tina Moreno. *A Teen's Guide To Living Drug Free*. Deerfield Beach, Fla.: HCI Teens, January 2003.

INTERNET ADDRESSES

A Guide for Teens
<http://www.health.org/govpubs/phd688/>
This guide from the U.S. Department of Health and Human Services gives tips for teens that may know someone with a drug or alcohol problem.

DEA: U.S. Drug Enforcement Administration
<http://www.dea.gov/>
Read about different operations that the DEA has enforced.

NIDA for Teens:
   The Science Behind Drug Abuse
<http://teens.drugabuse.gov/index.asp>
Learn about different drugs and more!

INDEX

57, 58–61, 64–68, 72–73,
75–76, 79–80, 81–88
  crystal, 11, 13, 20, 55
  effects of, 18–19, 20–21,
    22–23, 25, 27–31
  history, 33–35, 37–41,
    43–45
  street names, 15
  symptoms of a user, 30
  terminology, 87
  treatment, 75–88
  ways of using, 44
  yaba, 13, 20
Methamphetamine
  Anti–Proliferation Act, 43
methedrine, 34

N
National Clandestine
  Laboratory Seizure System,
  53
National Drug Intelligence
  Center (NDIC), 59–60
National Institute of Health,
  80
National Institute on Drug
  Abuse, 61
network therapy, 79

O
*Official Patient's Sourcebook
on Methamphetamine
Dependence*, 80
Operation Mountain
  Express, 11

Operation Northern Star,
  6–9, 13
overdose, 22, 37

P
paranoia, 18, 27, 29, 60
PC 1000, 48–49, 51
Proposition 36, 49–50, 51
pseudoephedrine, 5–7, 8, 9,
  11, 20

R
Royal Canadian Mounted
  Police (RCMP), 5, 11

S
Schedule II drug, 39, 40
"Speed Kills," 38
Substance Abuse and Mental
  Health Services
  Administration (SAMHSA),
  58–59
Substance Abuse Crime and
  Prevention Act, 50–51

T
trafficking, 6, 14, 43–44, 45
tweaker, 29, 31
twelve–step program, 77, 85

U
United States Department of
  Health, 38
United States Department of
  Health & Human Services, 13

W
weight loss, 30, 44, 59
withdrawal, 28–29